Celebrating Differences

Different Families

by Rebecca Pettiford

Bullfrog Books

Ideas for Parents and Teachers

Bullfrog Books let children practice reading informational text at the earliest reading levels. Repetition, familiar words, and photo labels support early readers.

Before Reading

- Discuss the cover photo. What does it tell them?

- Look at the picture glossary together. Read and discuss the words.

Read the Book

- "Walk" through the book and look at the photos. Let the child ask questions. Point out the photo labels.

- Read the book to the child, or have him or her read independently.

After Reading

- Prompt the child to think more. Ask: Think about your family. Now think of your best friend's family. How is your family like his or her family? How is it different?

Bullfrog Books are published by Jump!
5357 Penn Avenue South
Minneapolis, MN 55419
www.jumplibrary.com

Copyright © 2018 Jump! International copyright reserved in all countries. No part of this book may be reproduced in any form without written permission from the publisher.

Library of Congress Cataloging-in-Publication Data

Names: Pettiford, Rebecca.
Title: Different families / by Rebecca Pettiford.
Description: Minneapolis, MN: Jump!, [2018]
Includes index. | Identifiers: LCCN 2016054404 (print) | LCCN 2017015556 (ebook)
ISBN 9781624965470 (ebook) | ISBN 9781620316702 (hardcover: alk. paper) | ISBN 9781620317235 (pbk.)
Subjects: LCSH: Families—Juvenile literature.
Classification: LCC HQ744 (ebook)
LCC HQ744 .P48 2018 (print) | DDC 306.85—dc23
LC record available at https://lccn.loc.gov/2016054404

Editor: Jenny Fretland VanVoorst
Book Designer: Leah Sanders
Photo Researcher: Leah Sanders

Photo Credits: Getty: JGI/Tom Grill, 1; Portra Images, 4; Robert Deutschman, 6–7; Uwe Krejci, 12–13; Hero Images, 24. iStock: monkeybusinessimages, 5, 17; svetikd, 8–9, 10; Weekend Images Inc., 14–15; Paul Bradbury, 16. Shutterstock: pixelheadphoto digitalskillet, 3; Alena Ozerova, 11; Monkey Business Images, 18–19; DNF Style, 20–21; canovass, 22; goodlux, 23tr. SuperStock: Image Source, cover.

Printed in the United States of America at Corporate Graphics in North Mankato, Minnesota.

Table of Contents

Families are all different.

Tia has two dads.

Both put her to bed.

Both wake her up!

May has two moms.

One has brown hair.

One is blonde.

Both love her a lot.

Beth's mom and dad are divorced.

She is at her dad's house.

They have fun!

Beth's dad remarried.

Now Bea is her stepmom.

She has stepsisters, too!

11

Where does Ida live?

With her grandma.

Jay is adopted.

Mom cares for him all by herself.

Gia is adopted, too.
She was born in Korea.

PJ is her brother.

He is from Mexico.

Max lives with a foster family.

Soon he will be adopted, too!

What is your family like?

My Family

1. Get some paper and colored pencils. It's time to draw!
2. Draw a picture of the family you live with. Draw every person including yourself.
3. Who is each person? Who are they to you (mom, dad, stepmom, grandparent, sister, brother, etc.)?
4. Do you know another family? Draw a picture of that family.
5. How is that family different from yours?

Picture Glossary

adopted
To be raised by parents to whom one is not biologically related.

remarried
To be married again following a divorce or death.

divorced
A couple who has chosen to end their marriage.

stepmom
A woman married to one's father but who is not one's biological mother.

foster family
A family that cares for a child, usually until he or she is adopted.

stepsisters
Daughters of one's stepparent and his or her former partner.

Index

To Learn More

Learning more is as easy as 1, 2, 3.

1) Go to www.factsurfer.com

2) Enter "differentfamilies" into the search box.

3) Click the "Surf" button to see a list of websites.

With factsurfer.com, finding more information is just a click away.